Abigail Adams and the Women Who Shaped America

Torrey Maloof

Consultants

Katie Blomquist
Fairfax County Public Schools

Nicholas Baker, Ed.D.
Supervisor of Curriculum and Instruction
Colonial School District, DE

Publishing Credits

Rachelle Cracchiolo, M.S.Ed., *Publisher*
Conni Medina, M.A.Ed., *Managing Editor*
Emily R. Smith, M.A.Ed., *Series Developer*
Diana Kenney, M.A.Ed., NBCT, *Content Director*
Johnson Nguyen, *Multimedia Designer*
Torrey Maloof, *Editor*

Image Credits: Cover and p.1 LOC [LC-USZC4-4969]; cover, pp.1, 2–3, 4, 11, 12, 13, 14, 17, 23, 25 North Wind Picture Archives; pp.5, 9, 15, 16, 32 Collection of the Massachusetts Historical Society; pp.5, 26 (left) New York Public Library Digital Collections; p.6 Popperfoto/ Getty Images; p.7 (right) Granger, NYC, (left) LOC [LC-USZ62-1857]; p.10 (top) Glasshouse Images/Alamy, (center) LOC [LC-DIG-det-4a11321]; p.11 Journal of the American Revolution/Public Domain; p.13 LOC [LC-DIG-det-4a08438]; p.18 (front) NARA [299805], (back) U.S. Navy's Naval History and Heritage Command; p.19 DeAgostini/Getty Images; p.21 (top) LOC [LC-DIG-det-4a26203], (bottom) National Gallery of Art 1954.7.2; p.22 Beyond My Ken/Wikimedia Commons/CC BY-SA 4.0; p.23 Louis S. Glanzman/National Geographic/Getty Images; p.24 (left) Wikimedia Commons/Public Domain, (right) LOC [vc7.3p1]; p.25 U.S. Capitol/Public Domain; p.26 (right) Internet Archive/Public Domain; p.27 (right) Kenenth C. Zirkel/Wikimedia Commons/CC BY SA-3.0; (center) Sharon Mollerus/Flickr.com/CC BY 2.0; (left) Jixue Yang/ Dreamstime.com; all other images from iStock and/or Shutterstock.

Library of Congress Cataloging-in-Publication Data

Names: Maloof, Torrey, author.
Title: Abigail Adams and the women who shaped America / Torrey Maloof.
Description: Huntington Beach, CA : Teacher Created Materials, 2017. | Includes index.
Identifiers: LCCN 2015051131 (print) | LCCN 2016001683 (ebook) | ISBN 9781493830800 (pbk.) | ISBN 9781480756823 (eBook)
Subjects: LCSH: Adams, Abigail, 1744-1818--Juvenile literature. | Presidents' spouses--United States--Biography--Juvenile literature. | United States--History--Revolution, 1775-1783--Women--Juvenile literature. | United States--History--Revolution, 1775-1783--Participation, Female--Juvenile literature. | United States--History--Revolution, 1775-1783--Biography--Juvenile literature.
Classification: LCC E322.1.A38 M345 2017 (print) | LCC E322.1.A38 (ebook) | DDC 973.4/4092--dc23
LC record available at http://lccn.loc.gov/2015051131

Teacher Created Materials

5301 Oceanus Drive
Huntington Beach, CA 92649-1030
http://www.tcmpub.com

ISBN 978-1-4938-3080-0

Table of Contents

Putting Pen to Paper

Smoke filled the sky. The booming sound of cannon fire echoed through the air. At the top of Penn Hill stood a young mother with her seven-year-old son. She could not believe her eyes. She watched stunned as soldiers fought to their deaths. Some of those men were her friends. Others were her neighbors. She was heartbroken and distraught. The war was now too close to home.

People in Boston watch the Battle of Bunker Hill from their rooftops.

All Is Not Lost

The battle of Bunker Hill was an early battle that pitted the inexperienced American troops against the skilled British army. The Americans stood their ground until they ran out of **ammunition**. They did not win the battle. But they found hope.

That young mother was Abigail Adams. She was witnessing the Battle of Bunker Hill.

The next day, Abigail wrote to her husband, John. He was in Philadelphia. He and the other Founding Fathers were **debating** whether America should declare its independence. Abigail wrote, "My bursting heart must find vent at my pen." She told her husband about the battle she had witnessed. She wrote about a dear friend who had died in the battle. She explained that, "the constant roar of the cannon is so **distressing** that we can not Eat, Drink, or Sleep."

Abigail wrote many letters in her life. It is through these letters that we learn not only about the American Revolution but also about Abigail herself.

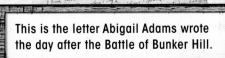

This is the letter Abigail Adams wrote the day after the Battle of Bunker Hill.

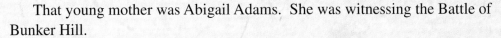

Abigail Adams

Before the War

Abigail Smith was born near Boston on October 11, 1744. She was raised on her family's farm. She had one brother and two sisters. Abigail was often sick as a child. But her illnesses did not hinder her curiosity. She loved to learn!

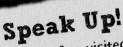

Speak Up!

People often visited the Smith home and talked about **politics**. Abigail was shy, but her father urged her to speak up and share her thoughts. This was a bit unusual. At that time, girls were mostly told to keep quiet.

Abigail's childhood home

colonial women

Back then, girls were not allowed to attend school. Even at a young age, Abigail felt this was unfair. She did not like that women did not have the same **rights** as men.

Despite this, Abigail received an education. Her mother taught her. Abigail learned how to write and do math. She also learned to read. Reading was one of Abigail's favorite things to do. She liked Shakespeare's plays. She studied history. She read about **philosophy** and law. But her mother worried. She thought Abigail was reading too much. But all that reading had made Abigail a very wise young woman. She would soon meet a man who would admire her wisdom.

A man named John Adams started visiting the Smith family home. He was a **lawyer**. A lawyer helps others with legal matters. When Abigail first met John, she was not impressed. She thought he was a bit ill-tempered and full of himself. It was not love at first sight for John, either. He thought Abigail was too quiet and awkward. But first impressions can be wrong, which proved true for these two.

John Adams

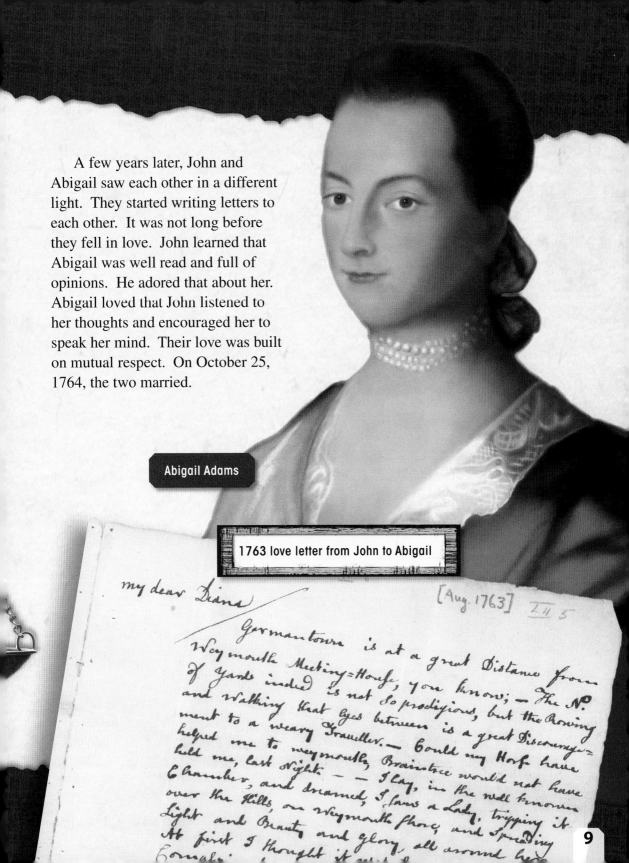

A few years later, John and Abigail saw each other in a different light. They started writing letters to each other. It was not long before they fell in love. John learned that Abigail was well read and full of opinions. He adored that about her. Abigail loved that John listened to her thoughts and encouraged her to speak her mind. Their love was built on mutual respect. On October 25, 1764, the two married.

Abigail Adams

1763 love letter from John to Abigail

After their wedding, Abigail moved to John's farm. Even though he was a lawyer, John came from a family of farmers. He still enjoyed working on a farm. Abigail grew to love farming, too. She churned butter and worked in the garden. She helped take care of the farm animals. Before long, the couple had children. Everything was going well for the family. But the world around them began to change.

In 1765, the British government passed a new law. The Stamp Act created a tax on printed items. Colonists now had to buy a stamp for items, such as newspapers and legal documents. That money went to the British government. Many colonists were angry, including John and Abigail. They thought the tax was unfair.

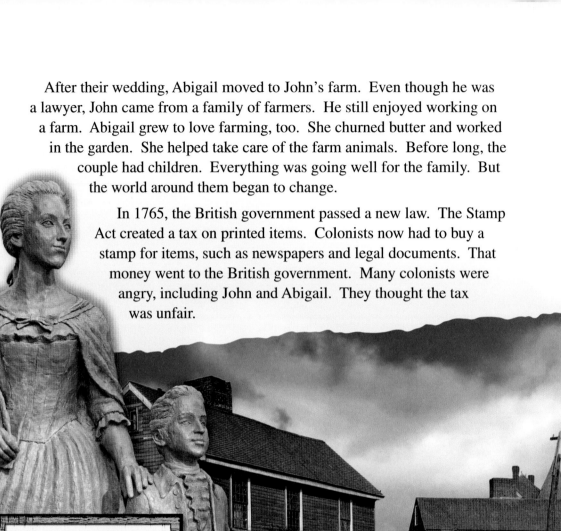

statue of Abigail Adams and her son John Quincy Adams in Quincy, Massachusetts

A Full House

Abigail and John had five children. The first was a daughter named Abigail, but they called her "Nabby." The second child was a son, John Quincy. He grew up to be the sixth president of the United States. They had another daughter, Susanna, and two more sons named Charles and Thomas.

John spoke out against the new tax. People listened. They agreed with him. In 1768, the Adams family moved to Boston. Now, John could be closer to his work. He was also closer to the action in the city. Boston was quickly becoming the center for British **resistance**.

A 1765 newspaper explains why colonists dislike the Stamp Act.

Colonists in New York speak out against the Stamp Act.

Tensions kept building in Boston. In 1773, the British government passed the Tea Act. This made it difficult for anyone but the British to sell tea in the colonies. Some colonists fought back. A group of men known as the **Sons of Liberty** dressed as Mohawk Indians. They snuck onto a ship in Boston Harbor. They dumped crates of British tea into the water. This event came to be known as the Boston Tea Party. Because of this act of **defiance**, Great Britain passed new laws. Most of them were aimed at Boston. One law closed its harbor. Another law limited the meetings town members could have. Boston was becoming a difficult and dangerous place to live.

Boston Tea Party

Homemade Tea

To protest the new tax, colonists **boycotted** British tea. They stopped buying it. Instead, they made their own. They called it *liberty tea*! Abigail made her own tea using berry leaves.

Soon, John was needed in Philadelphia. He was asked to attend the First **Continental Congress**. These were meetings at which leaders from the colonies discussed America's next steps. Should they declare independence? Should they start a war with Great Britain?

Abigail did not want to be alone in the city with her children. So, she moved back to the family farm. She worked hard to take care of the farm and her family while John was away.

Colonists meet to discuss their frustrations.

The First Continental Congress was held in Carpenters' Hall, Philadelphia, in 1774.

War Has Begun

In April of 1775, the American Revolution began. Abigail's life changed. From her home on the farm, she could hear battles raging around her. Many people fled Boston. They often stopped by her farm. She fed them and let them rest in her barn or her attic. Because of the war, supplies were short. Abigail did her part by making her own soap, ink, and cloth.

This woman spins her own thread to avoid buying British cloth.

During this time, Abigail wrote many letters to John. She told him what was happening around her. She let him know how hard the war was on her and the people she met. John shared her letters with Congress. He even showed some of them to George Washington! The letters helped the men see the toll the war was taking on people. It also showed them just how important their decisions were.

In this letter dated 1775, Abigail tells John about their friends and family while John is away.

Remember the Ladies

During this time, Abigail penned a famous letter to John. She wrote that she hopes to hear that America has declared independence. If America chooses independence, she knows that new laws will be needed. She then expresses her hopes for these new laws.

Abigail wanted rights for women. At that time, women had few rights. They had little power over their own lives. Abigail wrote that she wants laws that would protect women. She even told John that women may **rebel**, just like the colonists, if they do not get more rights. Abigail's ideas were ahead of her time. She was very insightful.

Abigail's "Remember the Ladies" letter

It was not long before Congress signed the Declaration of Independence. But Abigail's ideas about women's rights were not included. The men at the Congress disagreed with her. It would be another 100 years before the fight for women's rights would start to take shape.

Congress signs the Declaration of Independence.

After the War

The fighting finally ended in 1781. Abigail was happy, but she missed her husband. At this time, John was in Europe. He was trying to make peace with Great Britain. Abigail decided to visit him.

Abigail and her daughter, Nabby, headed for London. It took over a month for them to cross the ocean by ship. It was a hard journey. The seas were rough, and the boat was small. Both women suffered from seasickness. But it was well worth it when Abigail reunited with her husband.

This is the Treaty of Paris that officially ended the American Revolution in 1783.

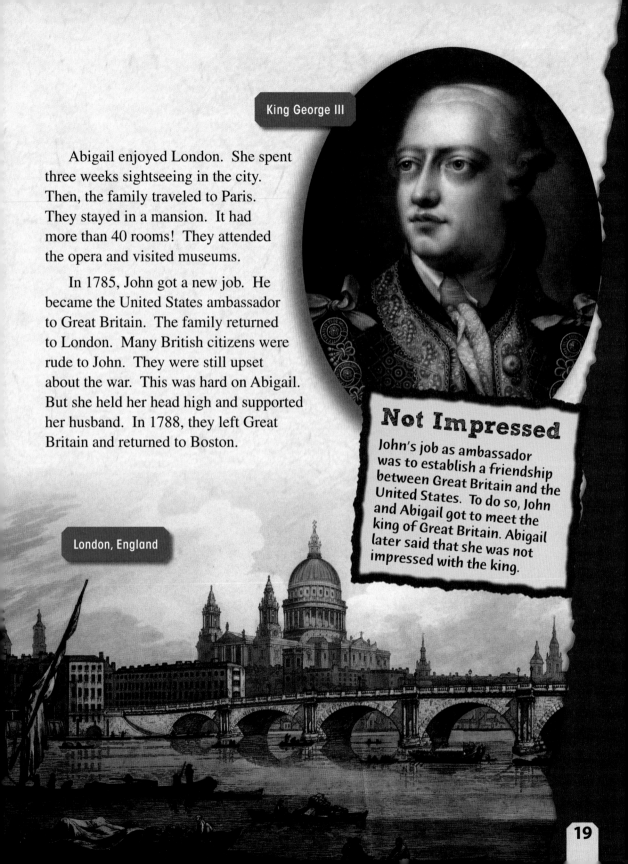

King George III

Abigail enjoyed London. She spent three weeks sightseeing in the city. Then, the family traveled to Paris. They stayed in a mansion. It had more than 40 rooms! They attended the opera and visited museums.

In 1785, John got a new job. He became the United States ambassador to Great Britain. The family returned to London. Many British citizens were rude to John. They were still upset about the war. This was hard on Abigail. But she held her head high and supported her husband. In 1788, they left Great Britain and returned to Boston.

London, England

Not Impressed

John's job as ambassador was to establish a friendship between Great Britain and the United States. To do so, John and Abigail got to meet the king of Great Britain. Abigail later said that she was not impressed with the king.

George Washington is sworn in as president with John Adams at his side.

Abigail was not in Boston long. In 1789, John was chosen to be George Washington's vice president. So they had to move to New York City. At this time, it was the capital. But they did not stay in New York long, either. Soon, the capital moved to Philadelphia.

When Washington decided not to run for president for a third term, many asked John if he would run. Abigail was not sure whether she wanted her husband to be president. He was older now. She knew it would be a difficult job. And, it would be very hard to fill Washington's shoes. Furthermore, she was tired. She was not sure if she wanted to be a president's wife. That was a tough job, too! In the end, John ran for office. And in 1796, he became the second president.

A Son Takes Office

Abigail and John happily lived out the rest of their lives on their farm. Abigail died on October 28, 1818. Sadly, Abigail did not live to see her son John Quincy Adams become president in 1825.

John Quincy Adams

Abigail and John moved to the new capital in Washington, DC. They were the first to live in the President's Mansion. Later, it would be known as the White House. During his presidency, John often asked Abigail for advice. And she happily gave it to him.

Abigail Adams

Heroines of the Revolution

Abigail was not the only woman who played a role in America's quest for independence. Many women helped America battle the British.

Margaret Cochran Corbin

Margaret and her husband, John, were **Patriots**. They wanted America to break free from Great Britain. John joined the Continental army. Margaret traveled with her husband. This was not that uncommon. Many wives went to war with their husbands. They cooked food for the troops and helped injured soldiers.

One day, John was loading a cannon. The man firing the cannon was killed. So John took over for him. Margaret stepped in and started loading the cannon. But then, John was killed, too. Margaret did not give up. She started firing the cannon herself. Margaret fought bravely in the battle. She was badly injured. But she survived.

This plaque honors Margaret's efforts in the war.

Sybil Ludington

You may have heard of Paul Revere, but have you heard of Sybil Ludington? She was only 16 years old in 1777 when she rode 40 miles through the rainy night. She alerted the local **militia**, or army, that the British were attacking a nearby town.

Molly Pitcher

Molly Pitcher is the nickname given to women who brought water to troops during the American Revolution. She was not a real person. But some think that Margaret may have inspired the nickname.

Mercy Otis Warren

Mercy was close friends with Abigail Adams. The two women had much in common. Even though neither woman received a formal education, they both enjoyed reading. They both spoke up for women's rights and liked talking about politics. Like Abigail, Mercy's husband worked in government. And both friends loved to write. Abigail is known for writing letters. Mercy is known for writing books, poems, and plays.

Mercy's plays focused on the politics of her day. This may have been because her brother and husband were active Patriots. The Sons of Liberty even had meetings at her home!

Mercy Otis Warren

This book by Mercy Otis Warren explains the history of the American Revolution.

The Founding Fathers draft the Declaration of Independence.

Mercy's plays were mainly **satires** that appealed to Patriots. She wanted America to declare its independence. She wanted to invoke patriotism. And she did just that. Her writing inspired others. It also influenced some of the most famous men of the day—the Founding Fathers! George Washington and Thomas Jefferson read her works. So did Patrick Henry and John Hancock.

advertisement for Phillis Wheatley's poems

Phillis Wheatley

Phillis was a slave. Her masters, John and Susanna Wheatley, saw that she was a bright girl. They made sure she received an education. When she was 12, she published her first poem. Then, she wrote a book of poems. She was the first African American to have her book published.

Women and the War

Abigail Adams was a unique woman. She was wise and caring. She was clever and liked politics. She loved her family. She also loved to write letters. It is because of these letters that we know so much about this remarkable woman's life. The letters serve as a window into her mind. They tell us her thoughts and feelings. And they show how history unfolded. They describe a war for freedom and independence.

During the war, Abigail showed bravery and commitment. She remained strong. She took care of her children. She helped her husband. She aided the people in her community. She did whatever she could to make a difference.

FAMILIAR LETTERS OF JOHN ADAMS AND HIS WIFE ABIGAIL ADAMS, DURING THE REVOLUTION.

WITH A

MEMOIR OF MRS. ADAMS.

BY
CHARLES FRANCIS ADAMS.

Publishing the Letters

Abigail's grandson published her letters in 1848. It had been 30 years since her death. The collection of letters was the first published work about a First Lady.

NEW YORK:
PUBLISHED BY HURD AND HOUGHTON.
Cambridge: The Riverside P___

Many other women helped America during the war, as well. Whether they used a pen or fired a cannon, these women made a difference. They fought for what they believed in. They showed what women are capable of. Abigail would have been proud of each of them.

This statue in Boston honors Abigail Adams.

Phillis Wheatley

Mercy Otis Warren

Mail It!

Abigail Adams enjoyed the art of letter writing. Now, write your own letter. First, research an event that took place during the American Revolution. You might research a battle, a British act, a revolt, or another event.

Then, write a detailed letter to a friend. Describe that event as if you were there. Describe the sights and sounds. Describe your emotions, too. Be sure to edit and proofread your letter. Write a final draft on nice stationery. Don't forget to mail it!

Glossary

ammunition—bullets and shells that are shot from weapons

boycotted—refused to buy, use, or participate in something as a protest

Continental Congress—meeting of colonial leaders to decide how to deal with Great Britain and to decide on laws

debating—discussing something with people whose opinions are different from your own

defiance—a refusal to obey an authority more powerful than you

distressing—suffering that affects the mind or body

lawyer—a person whose job is to help people in matters relating to the law

militia—regular citizens trained in military combat and willing to fight and defend their country

Patriots—people who supported American independence from Great Britain

philosophy—the study of ideas about knowledge, truth, and the meaning of life

politics—the ways in which governments and leaders do their work

rebel—to fight back against someone in charge

resistance—effort made to stop someone or something

rights—things that people should be allowed to have and do

satires—a form of humor that shows the weaknesses or bad qualities of a person, government, or society

Sons of Liberty—a secret organization of colonists who protested the actions of the British leaders

Index

Your Turn!

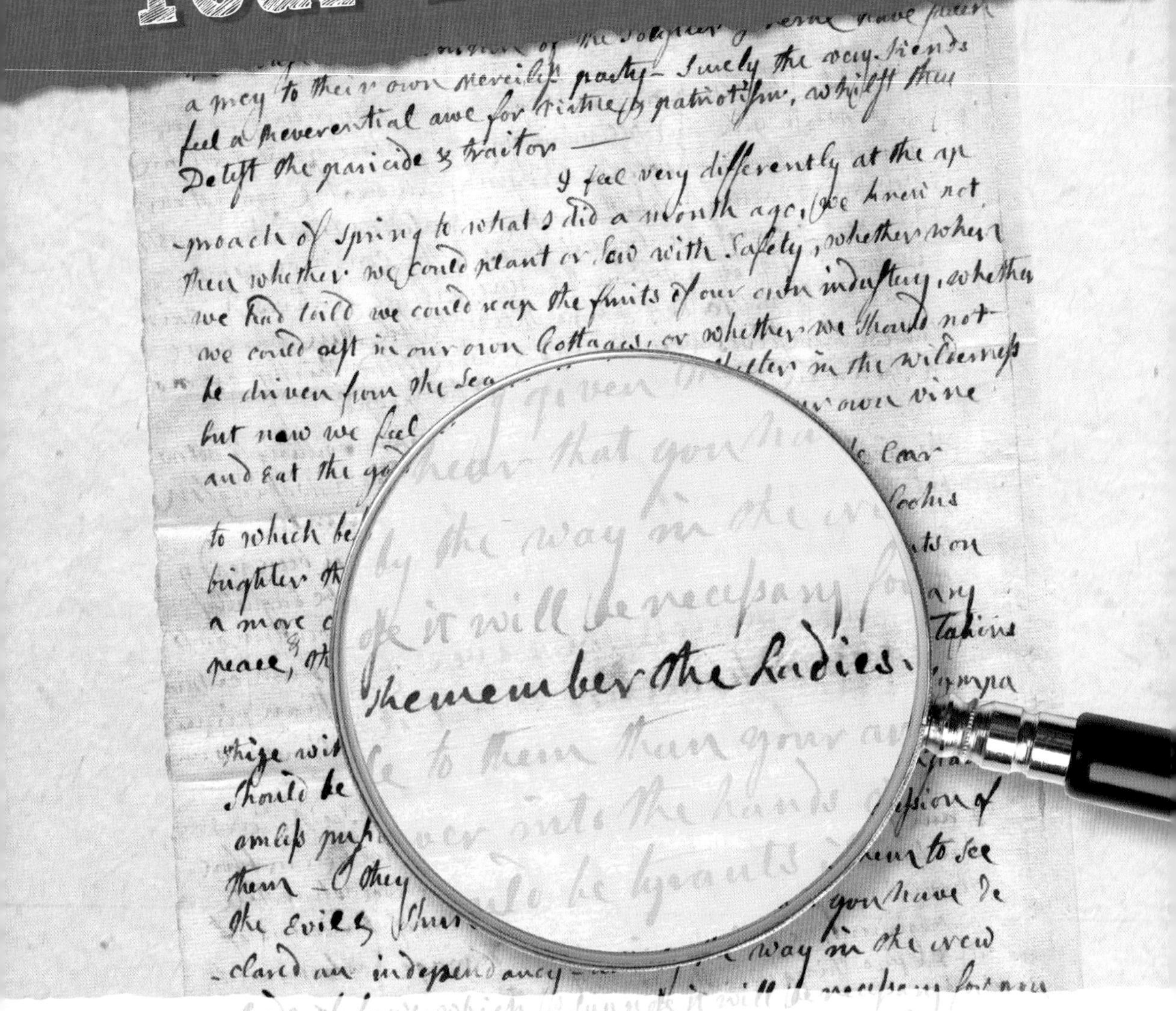

(handwritten letter text, partially visible through magnifying glass)

Remember the Ladies.

Remember Us, Too!

Abigail Adams asked her husband to "remember the ladies" in her famous letter. Write your own letter to John Adams. Ask him to remember a different group of people. Explain why this group is important.